LEAVING THE DOOR OPEN

LEAVING THE DOOR OPEN

Poems

By

David Ignatow

The Sheep Meadow Press

New York

ACKNOWLEDGMENTS

Grateful acknowledgment is made to the editors of the following publications in which these poems have appeared:

Virginia Quarterly, The Nation, Kenyon Review, Ploughshares, Poetry East, Poetry Now, Hampden-Sydney Review, Agni Review, Underground Rag Mag, Images, Manhattan Review, Boundary Two, Denver Quarterly, Amicus Journal, Colorado State Review, Paideuma, Confrontation.

Printed in the United States of America

The Sheep Meadow Press, New York, N. Y.

Distributed by Persea Books
225 Lafayette St., New York, N. Y. 10012

Library of Congress Cataloging in Publication Data

Ignatow, David, 1914–
   Leaving the door open.

   I. Title.
PS3517.G53L4   1984   811'.54   83-20237
ISBN 0-935296-52-2
ISBN 0-935296-51-4 (pbk.)

Arjuna Said: *Seeing my own kindred here, O Krishna,*
desiring battle, ranged against each other,
My limbs sink under me, my mouth dries up,
trembling besets my body, and my flesh creeps.

My bow Gandiva slips from my hand, my skin
burns with fever; I cannot stand, my heart
is confused;

I see contrary omens, O thou of the flowing
hair, nor can I look for the better part,
if I slay my kindred in battle.

Book 1, Bhagavad Gita

ALSO BY DAVID IGNATOW

Poems
The Gentle Weight Lifter
Say Pardon
Figures of the Human
Earth Hard: Selected Poems (1968)
Rescue the Dead
Poems 1934–1969
The Notebooks of David Ignatow
Selected Poems (1975)
Facing the Tree
Tread the Dark
Open Between Us (prose)
Whisper to the Earth

CONTENTS
Section One

Section Two

Section Three

Section Four

Section One

1.

He got his friends to agree to shoot him standing against a stone wall, somewhere in the country on a deserted farm. It was to resemble an execution, the plan cleared with the police, at whose headquarters he had signed attesting to his desire to be shot and, in clearing his friends, declaring his death a suicide that they were to help him to—at the peak of his strength.

Never to return to life in any form but that of earth itself, since earth was not fearful or joyous. And then he was followed, on inspiration, by his friends, one by one, each fired on by a diminishing squad until the last left was shot, as a courtesy by the police. Afterwards, the police shook their heads, puzzled, grieved and somehow angry at those bodies lying sprawled with outstretched arms and legs against the ground, as if pleading with the earth to let them in.

2.

Here comes one of my kind. It's night and I am caught in an open, deserted parking lot as I approach my car—a man, and I should not be afraid of what he may want to do to me, a man like me, with feelings of fear, hatred and love, and with a desire to live, like mine. I should greet him aloud as I would a long-lost brother or friend, recognizing him in the dark after all these years. I should feel good about it, welcoming his identity; and now if he is about to rob or perhaps kill me, I should smile at him, as he approaches.

3.

(For Neruda)

Soldiers surround the house of the poet and crouch, their guns poised in his direction, but do not move, held by their awe and fear in his presence. He comes to the window bitterly to look out upon his own people in uniform, with guns pointed at him. Bitterly he stands there and they, crouching, are more deeply silent in the anguish of their taut faces and eyes. He is their poet who speaks for them in his poems, that they have read and heard over and over, swaying to the rhythm of his lines.

He flings open the window where he is standing and shouts, Shoot, shoot me! They recoil in a body, except for one who with speed and reflex of long training at command raises his rifle and pulls the trigger. His comrades bury their faces in their hands.

4.

Two men wrestle on the ground.
Each one pinned beneath
can glimpse the stars
and the steep night,
friends lying dead beside him.
Whichever one lives will walk alone
past silent fields and houses.

As they pant and lunge for the throat,
rolling one on top of the other
across the ground, the fight grows
more formal, in contempt. They
have stared into the other's eyes
and seen one who can respond
to hatred or to love.

5.

I crawled over the dead bodies and moaning mouths of the dying to get to where my family was alive, hidden in its cave. I had been in search of food and firewood when I discovered I was in the midst of killers laughing and competing. I hid under a pile of dead heaped over me that I had dragged by the legs and arms to cover myself from head to feet, and I lay down, not breathing as the killers strolled by, jabbing idly with their knives at the dead to make certain. When the field grew silent, I slowly and cautiously made my way home on my belly, in case they in the distance looking back at their work could detect an upright, moving form.

Now I'm back with my wife and child, and we hug each other in silence from time to time, grateful to be alive, yet sick to our stomachs, unable to eat what I have foraged. Should we too die, we ask ourselves silently, looking into each others' faces? It seems so commonplace, after all those who fell like so many apples shaken from their boughs, but we drag ourselves over to the food and force ourselves to eat. Especially I urge my child, insist, command, threaten with punishment, and she submits, crying, and stuffs the berries into her mouth, chews sullenly and swallows.

6.

As he passes his hand over his face in front of the mirror in a gesture of weariness from the day's work, he sees he has wiped off the right cheek, with its bristle of hairs and its curves, to leave a solid as smooth as a billiard ball. He stares, wonders at how weary he must be to have to see this. He passes his hand over his left cheek, with the same result. He is alarmed at himself and questions his balance. To prove himself wrong in his suspicions, he runs his hand swiftly across his eyes, and they are wiped away, leaving him blind.

He screams, but he is alone. He would stare at his hand, but he cannot see; and he rushes madly out of the bathroom and into the living room, banging himself against the furniture. He is terrified of himself; his hand is his enemy, his destruction, and he holds it at a distance from himself rigidly, frozen in his fear, but in a burst of anguish he rubs his two hands together wildly, as if to wipe away the crime, and they wipe each other out, leaving him with two plugs of solid flesh resembling hooves.

He wishes to destroy himself, mad with grief. With the loss of his two hands, what worse can follow? And he passes the right plug of flesh across his head of hair in exhaustion and in horror he can feel the hair disappear beneath his touch. Insane now, he forces these flesh plugs to pass over each part of his torso and with each touch that part is wiped away. He laughs, out of his mind. He runs his plug down his legs and across his feet, and he falls to the floor with a crash, legs and feet giving way, no longer there. He begins to flop on the floor like a fish cast upon shore. The door to his apartment opens and his wife enters, observes him tossing himself about, tangled up in his clothes, and is silent.

8

7.

The sweetness in a man, the very one about to set out to kill a stranger in the forest for poaching his preserves of wild animals, vegetation and fruits: he plays upon his clay pipe melodies about himself: his love for children, wife, tribe and land. It sets others to listen, nod and glance at one another knowingly and to focus on him the more closely to hear how he reaches them in their feelings about themselves and their affections. He gathers spear and sword in his hands and steps softly into the woods to kill. He grinds his teeth in expectation of killing with a fury that will brook no resistance of the creature he is after to make it die in its blood.

Later, he will take up his clay pipe to play in the knowledge that he has killed one that delighted too in the fruit and vegetables of the forest and who loved having been born into its offerings. He will play and perhaps call it a prayer to the mystery of having to live and die in a surrounding of plenty that never in itself will die, as if to dream one could take from it the power in food to live forever but for some baffling reason is never to happen. As he plays, suddenly, because he cannot solve the mystery of his own eventual disappearance, perhaps by the spear of his enemy, if not age—suddenly, in frustration with the question, he will begin to dance, to dance out the disappointment in thinking, in questioning, in searching in himself for an answer. He will dance unto exhaustion, and all who have been listening to him play since the beginning, startled to see him rise to his feet to dance, will join him, his bafflement theirs, as it conveyed itself to them in his playing from the beginning.

8.

This newspaper states that Idi Amin killed over one hundred thousand Ugandans last year. How did we manage to do that, Idi? I am an ordinary man, I enjoy my food; I love to make love. How did I manage to kill that many? I remember, calm now, at peace with myself after a fine meal, my violent temper, my tantrums, my sudden turn to cold calculation to kill those tribes—men who oppose my rule. Not openly but by practicing rites forbidden them. They raise gods and magical powers above my rule. I cannot be threatened. I am growing furious again.

How many have we killed, Idi? I have here a report that these same rites continue to be practiced in the bush. Hunt those people down, I command; slaughter every one of them. Pull out their fingernails; crush their balls in your hands, and women—crush their breasts between your fingers until they burst. I am Idi Amin. And bring me my wife; I want to make love again to forget those fools who would oppose me. I have to shake my head. I am a man like all men.

•   •   •

Idi, I dance with the dancers, sing their songs, drink their wine and mingle among them with my broadest smile. I enjoy the wine and comradeliness of bodies with which I feel at one, of my kind—men, and any one, as I look him in the eye, I barely restrain myself from shooting, so much do I fear him too, who would kill me to take my place.

Idi, the dancing increases in violence and meaning. I watch myself dance in their bodies, and I know I am frightened of myself in their bodies, as they are frightened of me in their tumultuous rhythms, but I am, and I am who must live myself.

10

Dancers dismissed. Guards, surround me; I am returning to the palace to brood on death.

Here in the palace, Idi, I ask myself why do I think this way, and I answer myself reassuringly: power is beauty and beauty is what I am after, that which I feel in my marrow when I exert power. Then I transcend myself, I become the power, and I kill to make my beauty blaze.

I forgive myself, there is no one to take my place, for I am; therefore, I must be Idi Amin.

9.

He is searching inside his body for the cause of his depression. It's as if he were searching with his hand from organ to organ in his chest. He can feel depression near his heart, but as he moves ever so cautiously in and around that area to grasp that ache and extract it, nothing comes to hand.

He conceives of it as something living within him illegitimately, and, since he cannot remove it bodily and has addressed his plea to it more than once to remove itself from him, he believes that now he has the right to do it violence, to drown it, and he begins to drink.

He becomes a fog to himself, the heavy mist that rises from his drink in conflict with the inner warmth, and he no longer can detect specific depression. It is now a general fog and that, of course, is as nature can be in unstable conditions. He thinks himself a fact of nature, and he travels unsteadily, as fogs do, from street to street, from house to house and, like fog, finds himself locked out from these houses or hurried past.

It is night. Fog, through which all things must enter and pass, can be dangerous. Vehicles are traveling at high speed, and fog is pierced by lights, by people and by trucks. He is knocked down and crushed. As mountains are shaken and torn down and earth opens, his death too is a phenomenon in nature. Affirmed in his being, he rolls over on his face to die.

Section Two

10.

My uncle smoked his cigarettes down to the last half inch and served cherry jelly with crackers and tea on Sunday to his guests. He was methodical about costs. And I used to climb the tree for the cherries. The crackers and jelly were hard to come by in quantity for my hunger. Just a handful of biscuits on a plate and one small jar that made the guests feel greedy after two helpings. Uncle would look on approvingly and smile and praise his jelly, homemade off the cherry tree. No sugar on the table for the tea, not with jelly.

As for his wife, hands folded in her lap, she sat apart without comment, for her husband knew how to make money, a stubborn man for bread and cheap cuts and so there was cash for mortgages in the neighborhood: old-law tenements and clapboard, two-family structures with worn wooden steps. Their landlords came to his hardware store for supplies to be charged double for postponing the interest on their mortgages.

On Sunday it was all family, in summer especially. Everyone sat at the round, green, cracked table between the garden and the back entrance to the store, a concrete patio with straight-back, round-bottomed cane chairs. My father and Uncle Philip and Aunt Bessie, my mother and Aunt Pesha and Uncle Hymie and cousins Archie, David, Frieda, Fay, Dora, Bertha and Alex—together running in and out of the garden, climbing up the tree, pushing the lawnmower across the grass and eating the crackers and jelly. I was hungry for food but, my father heatedly defending the democratic cause in the last war, my uncle's wisecracks interested me, he who owned the garden and the store.

11.

Here in bed behind a brick wall
I can make order and meaning,
but how do I begin? How do I
emerge without panic
to the sounds and mass
of people in the street?

Are they human who stare
as I pass by, as if sizing me up
for a mugging or a filthy proposition,
and am I human to have to be
frightened and on guard?

It's people I'm afraid of, afraid
of my own kind, knowing their angers
and schemes and violent needs, knowing
through knowledge of myself
that I have learned to resist,
but when I can't I have seen
the havoc I have made.

It's this, knowing their desperate motives,
as I have known mine, I'm afraid of
in them. I hide upon a bed
behind a brick wall and listen
to engines roaring up and down
the street and to voices shouting
to one another and find no meaning
or order in them, as there is none
in me when I am free of self-restraint.

The bed is my victory over fear.
The bed returns me to my self
as I was young and dreaming
of the beauty of the trees
and faces of people.

12.

I find you at twenty-six
seeking refuge
in drugs and hospital routine,
the same son I raised in anger
and self-pity who is without hope
of a life free of me and I know
we both are in trouble.

13.

I no longer want to feel with you
your tragedy—if but for a moment
to experience death. That cannot
bring home a salary, a toy
for my child, a poem to tell
of my life with or without you.
I will be known for the steadiness
with which I carry grief,
so that one could use me
as a pillar for a house.
And since this tragedy is for us both
you will see me in the distance
walking firmly, so that you
will want to follow,
leaving death behind.

14.

Stranger in my life,
I will take care of you
even after my death—to whom
I give the feeling of a father
to his grieving son, for whom
the father will do anything
to make him live.

                Stranger,
the cause of my bitterness
at your condition, and my strange pride,
you my son since no one else
comes to claim you and since I
am sworn to myself to give you all
a father can: love, pity and faith.

15.

You are totally helpless in sleep
and yet I cannot enter your thoughts
or your innermost desires
as they're evoked in dreams.
We remain apart and I am a man
lonely with himself and in need
of another.

I fold my hands in my lap
and wait for resignation
to announce itself in me
and with it an acceptance
of another self that writes
this observation in silence
and in pity.

16.

I named you my son, then withdrew
and you have been searching for me
ever since, with anguish and confusion.
Here I am, you think, reaching out
and catching yourself, about to fall.

17.

Whatever contribution I was to make to living
has been made, yet living has gained nothing
from it but a sharpened sense of its futility
for me. The robin hops from branch to branch
as if one branch makes a difference over the other
and hopping in itself is important to the cause.

•   •   •

Standing idly at the door to the meadow,
not knowing of anyone in need of me,
made unwanted to myself, I glimpse
my neighbor standing in his doorway
too and staring out.

18.

The dog's bark that sounds as though it were choking
on its own grief, I hear it nearly every night
before bed and take it into sleep
to be used, I know, to name a part
I would prefer to lose—that part
I won't recall except reluctantly,
as if I were to face myself in something
hopeless of correction, yet must be felt
again because I am the guilty one
for wanting to escape that grief—
unhappy, coughlike bark at night,
and night is dark enough to keep it hidden,
but night is when it happens
and where it lives.

19.

There is a fault in the universe
that I should have the fault of self-doubt.
The constant exploding outwards
into space, as if to occupy it all
to leave no room for doubt.

If there's no end to space,
then there is no end
to explosiveness, and to racing outwards.
With space finite, the universe
will turn in on itself, crushing
each particle of self in search
of assurance, constancy, stability.

20.

What kind of life is it for a bird that lands upon a branch alone, followed directly on its heels by another, with cries of delight or anger between them, a sort of scuffle I hear, as in an attempt at mating—and away flies the bird that followed, leaving the other by itself, alone again perhaps to perch in its aloneness. It too suddenly flies off and pierces the air in the silence to a new branch or whatever.

Where then is the flock with which to join up and be consoled, or what is it that birds do to fortify each other in their desolation? Is it instead this aloneness, and for that bird, too, that followed in the silence of a hot afternoon of sky as clear, as firm-looking as blue marble?

21.

Lying quietly on the bed
I've become an object of the room
the way my book in hand exists
from moment to moment, its contents fixed.

How lovely it is to exist as an object.
How sweet and tranquil are the filing cabinets
and ceiling. I have found in myself
their separation from thought: never confused
in themselves or seen by others as anything
but what they are
to the touch and to the eye.

22.

The language among the clashing winds
and falling trees is action, unexplained
to me or to themselves and unmediated
by feeling for or against—neither
open to discussion with others
nor with themselves. That leaves me
tongue-tied and in a hurry
to secure my safety within
my house, and the trees bend
ominously towards it
beneath the violence of the wind.

No, it's no use longing
for lyric joy, sorrow or fear. It's
no use longing for words of love
or pleading. It's simply to act
as do the trees or the wind:
to become an agent of that force
that could save my life,
and so I become impersonal to myself,
a mind of the wind.

23.

The bird was flying towards me
from a distance and as it drew near
to where I stood watching
from behind the deck window
it veered off into the woods
as if I were a stranger
among the grass and flowers.

One bird giving me an insight
into its reasoning
could make me feel at home.

Section Three

24.

How the zebra died in the mouth
of the lioness after a brief struggle
of the legs, and then the herd went back
to feeding on the grass nearby
while the lioness and her cubs knelt
at the body as in worship
and ate their fill.

They were soon quiet and resting
on their full bellies and looking
steadily at the herd feeding itself
with heads down to the grass,
not minding the lioness or her cubs.

It was a reassuring sight,
that there was death
and that it had its place
among the living, and a time,
and that time had passed
for now.

25.

The dog barks and is for the moment a dog heard.
The child cries and is for the moment a child heard.
Also, there is the lover swearing his oath.
Silence falls on each, and the thousands
of dogs, children and lovers pass by silently.
They could be shadows.

                     There is no turning
each to the other: "We are all lovers,
love me in return; we are all children,
love me as a child," or "We are all dogs,
let us bark together in that pleasure."
They are stilled to have found themselves
among their own kind in troops of thousands,
and when one dog barks or a lover speaks
his oath or a child cries, it is passed over
as an anomaly, a pretense
at being a dog or lover or child.

26.

You are unhappy with the way things
have turned out for you and for others
close whose lives touch yours
and turn it from its path in the sun.
You are now with your back to it
and looking down at your shadow
stretching before you
at your feet, long, dark and sad
and you make of it a matter
for philosophy.

27.

The steam hammer pounds with a regularity on steel I should envy. Neither the hammer nor the steel seems to be suffering from this terrible meeting between them, proving something vaguely pointed, that some things must be done, regardless of cost, and finally the cost too is absorbed in the doing that has become a ritual between two fated opponents.

28.

He has come to the conclusion,
walking between the empty lot
and the stone heap, his arms filled,
that this is the life. Stones fall
from his loaded arms and bruise
his feet. He trips. He could
pick flowers, he could heap his arms,
but with stones there is
always the danger,
the need to be alert.

29.

How good it is to feel the joy at last
of oneself. It is like the full moon
shining down upon the dark trees. It is
like the lit trains sliding by in the dark.
It is the light of houses in the distance
punctuating the night.

30.

He is hobbling along on a wooden leg, with cup out-stretched, seeking compassion and love for partnership in his grief at his crippled condition, each penny dropped into the cup a token that he can treasure and add to the sum needed.

Very little is offered, a penny at long intervals by someone who seems more concerned with his own state of mind, as if reminded of an unspoken, unacknowledged guilt, some lack in himself uncovered. The man with the wooden leg keeps limping along. At least, he thinks, he is among people and is not being removed and isolated by a cop, and he can guess that this is the real and secret offering, the tacit knowl-edge that he belongs; that if love, compassion and partner-ship are what he seeks, he is receiving them from many silent eyes that look in passing, letting his image sink into their thoughts like a penny.

31.

Wherever he looks, standing still in the city,
are people born of coupling, walking in grey suits
and ties, in long dresses and coiffed hair,
speaking elegantly of themselves and of each other,
forgetting for the moment their origin,
perhaps wishing not to know or to remember.
They dress as if having been born in a clothing store.

They were born of men and women naked
and gyrating from the hips
and with movements up and down
and with climactic yells,
as if losing their lives
in the pleasure and so glad,
so wildly glad.

From this rises the child
from between the wet crotch, blood and mucous.
He stands upright and pronounces himself
humankind and steps from bed and clothes himself
in a grey suit and from the next room of birth
steps a woman in a long dress. They meet
in the corridor and arm in arm walk its length
in search of one room, empty of inhabitants
but prepared for them.

32.

He was caressing the back and shoulders
of the woman seated beside him, his head
turned towards me in conversation, when
this woman started from his caress
and observed quite casually she was not
his wife, who without his knowledge
had changed her seat and was laughing
at him from across the room.

33.

At table they talked of family and kids,
of friends and happenings and argued versions
of the world and of events they read about
or had experienced together. They found it hard
to reach agreement on the issues and let them
fall away in silence as they ate. They were
together not to quarrel or to discuss
but to seek to make a wholeness
with each other and wholeness was the silent issue
they would not debate, since nothing else
could substitute for two together
and then they talked of love and sex
and there agreed, not saying so,
how they together were expressed in this
and so they quipped and teased
and silently agreed to go to bed,
with dinner done, and there perform
the rites of two, freed of loneliness
to make themselves the host to each other.

34.

They came at him with crooked teeth;
he had over his eyes, it seemed, the film
of the newborn, who sees objects as emblems
of light moving upon the film's surface.
His senses pleased by light and such symbols
that announced it, he followed it devotedly,
sensing form that sought his attention
persistently above all others, in hovering
over him, in offering him objects from its hand:
gifts, some filling his mouth with sweetness,
others eliciting a joy for their guessed-at
usefulness to him. In the forms swelling
to meet him, in the eyes that were soft
to rest his gaze upon, he sensed a portent
of pleasure greater than any he had yet attained.
It was disturbing for what he sensed
of the pleasure such softness emphasized.
He was not loath to accept, his eyes still filmed.
There was light and light glowed
and with but light to go by he too shone.

He first felt their teeth when they came at him
quite close, breathing upon his cheek.
He had no fear of that. He preferred it,
and then their teeth as they pressed upon him
ripped open this film. Light was not lost by it.
Light remained and grew explicit at last
in the sight of strands of hair and foggy teeth
parted by gaps. He had no revulsion.
He was excited by particulars. Light
held everything as before but not everything
was an emblem; the shapes were not of the light
but distinct organs revealed. He examined
these revelations for detail to satisfy

his new wonder, and there was this new thought
pieced together of these details: they
were organs working together to form one object.
He had no revulsion towards this object.
He was instead drawn to it for the continuity
he now needed to establish for always,
as he had established light at the beginning,
these differences: these strands of hair,
these parted, creased lips, those foggy teeth.

He learned to love them as he loved light
for they were what made light transcendent
by being form and volume. He learned to consider
them as darkness, delightful; they gave comfort
by touch. His film gone, he believed now
in comfort, and light being everywhere
as the disturber: it belonged to nothing
yet was everywhere. Now that the film was gone
light was not all happiness, and the details
of an object were more restful to contemplate,
and he has called them in approval, darkness.

35.

Outside his window a woman washes her window
so that sitting alone she may look through
and be seen clearly. If he should turn his back
still she would be there
as he would be to her
and she would accept his back
as that part of himself
that by its nature has nothing
to say to her but presence.

Neither one of them is ever alone
in a sense that could be frightening,
such as facing the stars
in an empty meadow, with no one
aware of one's presence, with no one
curious about one's absence
so that one does not exist, except
in one's own mind that is frightened
of itself in a silent meadow
facing the stars that to themselves
are adequate.

36.

Here he is, sitting quietly, enjoying
his own presence, for it turns out
from many quarrels and separations
in himself has come an understanding
that he is the one
with whom to sit at peace silently
in friendship, or to converse.

37.

He is digging his own grave a little while before he expects to die. After all, it will be his last residence and he has always built his own before. He does not want to be carried in a coffin. He will walk when he senses himself dying, and will climb down into the grave and stretch out, with people looking on: relatives, friends, creditors and those indebted to him. He will have forgiven them their debts, again to show himself free, since to die does not mean to become a tree root, or simply food for the mice. It is a stage one comes to, as at the end of a friendship or love affair when either lover or friend moves out, leaves the country or moves elsewhere. There will be that same change within, or in the grave, if he can no longer detect this change, it will be change nevertheless, and change is what he always knew above ground.

Did he always recognize himself, as when before the mirror he found himself growing aged and could not connect that with his once youthful, full face, but he was aware, and now he can expect the change that will come without his being conscious of it, but he knows of this change; he is informed. Do we not make chairs and tables of living trees? And he hauls up a large chunk of dirt with his shovel.

38.

I am a vase holding a bunch of flowers
in my depth, with water in it. I enjoy
the branches leaning against my sides.
They make me feel myself.

See how tall and straight I stand
with blossoms above me. Could anything
be more beautiful than I who am nothing
but an enclosure upon emptiness?

Section Four

39.

Do you know I love you?

What can I do about it?

Doesn't it make you feel good to know?

No, I don't love you.

Then why not enjoy the thought that I'm in love with you?

If that makes you feel better. . . I've got troubles of my own.
I too want to love someone. I don't mean to hurt you, but
you're not my type.

I see. What is your type?

Oh, I don't know. He has to come on in a funny way, maybe
look at me or say something suddenly that gets to me. I
have to suddenly realize that this is the man I want.

Is he tall or short, dark-haired or blond?

I wish I knew. I'm just waiting for him to come along.

And then what will happen?

I'll be happy.

I'll be glad for you.

Thanks.

And when I find someone else instead of you—it hurts me
to say it, it's hard to believe, I don't want to believe it has
to be anyone else but you—you'll congratulate me, too.

I sure will. I'll be very happy to see you happy.

We'll both be happy, won't we?

Right.

And we'll be able to talk to each other so friendlylike and intimately about each other's happiness.

Yeah.

Whom do you think I ought to fall in love with again instead of you?

Oh, I don't know. It could be someone you like, I guess.

It would have to be, or I couldn't fall in love. Well, can you picture with whom I could fall in love?

Probably someone like me again who has a different feeling about you from what I have.

I wish I knew where to find her. Imagine finding someone just like you. I could dream all the time it was you, who had decided I was the guy, after all, who had come along suddenly to make you feel that something different.

Yeah, that would be funny.

Do you know anyone who looks like you?

No.

I don't either. How about you acting that role for me? Let me hear how it would sound.

What do you mean?

Just pretend that you suddenly found in me the man you want and act it out.

How do I do that?

Oh, I don't know, just act. Haven't you ever pretended anything?

Sure.

Well, that's it.

You mean put my arms around you and coo into your ear and all that?

Yeah. I want to see what it would be like to have someone like you in love with me.

That's crazy.

Yeah, but it would be fun for me, at least. Here, take this arm and place it around my shoulder and this arm around my waist. And now say something in my ear.

Like what?

Oh, anything, something soft and nice.

You playing some kind of game? I'm not in love with you, remember.

I didn't forget. Sure I'm playing a game. I want someone like you in love with me, and you're playing the role. Now you have to kiss me.

What if I don't?

Then I'll be terribly unhappy again and won't have you to help me imagine that I finally found my girl.

But what about me, looking for my man to love me?

O.K., I'll pretend to be that man. Then kiss me, too.

You know what? This isn't too bad, you and me like this.

Let's keep it up.

O.K., let's keep it up, and we'll make each other happy, pretending that I have the man and you the woman you love forever. At least I know you love me, so I have that to bank on.

And you're satisfied to stay with me for the moment.

Maybe longer. Who knows?

And I have that to bank on.

You know what? I think we're both happy.

Let's go to my house.

I'd better pack my things.

That was a real problem, and look how easily we solved it.

By putting our heads together.

40.

My hot-water bottle, my latest love,
when it grows cold I won't have any sad feelings
because I'll know I need only pull out the stopper
in its head and pour out the cold
and pour in the hot. My ideal love.
It couldn't possibly leave me, either,
and when I grow tired of it I can put it aside
and forget it and the bottle would never mourn
or make me feel guilty.

But what when it springs a hole in its side
and begins to leak? Then I'll think
it does not want to stay with me any longer;
that it wants to be left alone
to grow old and rot and be thrown
on the garbage heap, and I'll be sad for it
and have to think of getting a new hot-water bottle.
I'll be the one who will mourn
and the bottle will be left with no feelings
towards me at all. You can't win.

41.

I'm lying in bed looking up at the ceiling,
asking what are the limits to pleasure,
as I feel rising within a need
to grasp a hand in my hand
for its firmness and form,
our faces turned up to see clouds
and sunlight merging, then sailing apart:
beauty and then rupture,
as it is within our grip upon each other—
to make of it that kind of love
between two selves that must break apart
to be what they are.

42.

Everyone touch everybody's lips. It's ritual, it's important. Now form a circle, everyone, and look at each other. What do you see? Another person, naturally, but what else? You see yourself through the eyes of another. You see yourself as another, and these crosscurrents of sight meet and would cancel in passing through but are stopped to become entwined, tense knots of air.

You are not a woman, as the woman opposite looks at you, and you are not about to imagine her a man. You would wish she were one to make things easier between you.

If only you were a woman, she is thinking. How much easier life could be for both, but the knot of air stays tense between you, and you have to smile because there is no other way to ease and dissolve the tension; you are each as you are, so you step forward out of the circle and hold out your hand. She promptly follows with outstretched hand, and to your surprise, it happens with each person in the circle, each holding the hand of another, a hand no different from your own. You could be holding hands with yourself, but the voice speaking to you is another's, and this difference is what interests you to go on being yourself talking and loving.

43.

Sadly is how I must say it
because I am one brother
and you one sister. Together
we fade into the crowd
of many faces awaiting our bed.

Should we not become many happinesses,
many starts of love and elated deaths?
My body weakens into the milky dawn
and grows pale with effort. You
already are dressed and moving about,
a person with a coffeepot. I
stick out my tongue to touch
the brightening sky.

44.

Finally, I have reduced you to a human being.
I have recovered my own humanity,
as you concede quietly. I listen and am sad.
We are two mirrors standing opposite
each other, in one another's reflection.

Where is your first experience
of ruling me with your eyes,
you who must be looking for me
behind my eyes and my reserve
only to find that I am once again
a disappointment, as we are to ourselves.
I am my own small independency
and you the kingdom of yourself.
We meet to form a treaty of respect
and commonality, touching
at the borders of each other's self,
our bodies meeting on a bed.

45.

The men you've loved are one man,
the women I've known are one woman;
I hold your hand and look
into your face with love, in peace.
We lie down together
and nothing matters
but making each of us
the first and the last.

46.

What we have done to keep a good house
and an orderly one: loved strangers,
even those who came to muddy up the floors;
loved them in place of commotion,
the sooner to be rid of them
or to find in them a spot
of their own cleanliness—as love
would hypnotize us to believe,
and once rid of those who have gained
theirs in getting love from us, we
cleaned up again: recalled their pleasures
and our discoveries.

All this, taking our strength day after day,
has left us, the central idea, in possession
of a new fact: that we are old in the work:
we falter at the windows
and seek to hire help, friends,
whose payment is to take all.

47.

Air that embraces me in a gentle breeze
is just as intent at that moment on touching
the lips, feet and arms of the population
of the world. Oh anybody's whore whom we love,
nevertheless; who makes amoral persons
of us all. Hitler slept with and was touched
by air and every escaped assassin and bank robber,
every double-crossing politician and racist
stretches himself luxuriously each morning
in bed in the summer air through his open
inviting window.

What shall we do with such an indiscriminate
being that teaches us to be unfaithful
to our wives, husbands and lovers,
and that so many of us take as inspiration
to follow our new-found morality
with a passion? As for me, in view of such
practices as air induces, immune to punishment
or retribution or unhappiness with itself,
I lift a hand to caress the cheek
of my own special beloved and dream
large, world-throbbing dreams.

48.

The glow upon the ground
beneath the tree that lets the sun
come through in spots like sun
upon a brown-skinned woman partly
shaded by a tree—she turns to show
her sunlit teeth in welcome
to her lover approaching. She sees him
as a tall stalk of grain striding
above the field. He wraps his leaflike arms
around her waist, and she her sunlit arms
around his neck, and thus they stand
until evening falls, until night fades
into dawn, until the sun rises. They
are as one with earth.

49.

A leaf spirals directly at the tall grass
without wavering or hesitation, as if knowing
in advance where it must go. And now it lies
hidden in the grass, not stirring, content
with itself, I would say, having left the tree
to find itself a place on earth.

50.

I did not take into account my disillusionment, I looked to overlook it, to throw myself into new life, and there you were about to be born. Now you are grown and, as it seems, look at me in my guilt, to ask, "Why did I have to be born? Why could I not have stayed with the earth, the clouds, the sun and the moon? Why am I a part of this restlessness, tears and striving for what I do not know?" I can't answer, I have no answer. I could confess myself deluded about the new life I was to start, at your birth, and you then would mock and call me self-centered, an egotist who thought nothing of giving pain to another. I would have to acknowledge my fault, and you would weep that I am wishing you were never born, and so I would be caught in the irony of not being permitted to tell the truth. I remain silent. I bend my head. I could say, "We'll push through, we'll manage, we'll survive, we'll do everything to make ourselves happy." And you would smile gladly, ready to deceive yourself also. We would be implicated together in the great lie and carry on with humor about ourselves and find reason for living in laughing at ourselves, and so to look at each other in recognition and affectionate contempt.

51.

How was it possible I was a father
yet a child of my father? I grew
panicky and thought of running
away, but knew I would be scorned
for it by my father, and so I stood
and listened to myself being called
Dad.

How ridiculous it sounded
but in front of me, asking
for attention—how could I
as a child ignore this child's plea?
And so I lifted him
into my arms and hugged him
as I would have wanted my father
to hug me, and it was as if
satisfying my own lost childhood.

52.

It is annihilation of the person you became in meeting people who cannot exist for you in your room. You shed them painfully and are frightened, left with the person you were, this with whom you are now, composed of fear and doubt setting you adrift. You are nowhere in particular and do not know that you exist except as these feelings. It is the end of you personally, become the ocean of your feelings. Fish are in that water: sharks and whales and all other manner of living fins and tails.

Is it a giddy moment for you to have become an ocean in your small, private room? Nothing more can be said until you learn what whales and sharks and other moving fins do in your waters, for they could not exist without your feelings having become oceanic and a nourishment for other life than your lost one—then to have discovered this life in you become a festive occasion.

53.

The machine, you know, will vary with the weather.
Since iron and steel are products of the earth,
why should they not alter with the atmosphere?
Be kind to your machine, then, as to your dog
or self. In sun or rainy weather do not ask
the same results of it, and do not push it
too far and fast. One tiny screw binding
air rod to valve will break as if by accident
in your hand. Do not believe it an accident
merely, but a warning, and then shut down
the motor, let the machine cool off
and slowly, very slowly, replace the broken
with the new. Be sure the threads are clean,
do not force. Try it gingerly at the tip.
Do not resist if it balks and try again
with another but be careful, be careful
always of this created thing. It knows you.

54.

What's your name?

What does it matter to you?

Because I have a ticket for you.

What kind of ticket?

Well, I can't tell you unless I know your name.

But how can my name have any bearing on the ticket?

Well, it could change with your name.

Are you crazy?

No, my name is Sam.

Then I'm crazy.

Oh, so that's your name. Well, the ticket I have is for you to appear at Bellevue at 3 P.M. sharp to have your head examined.

What for?

Didn't you say you're crazy?

But not that way.

What other way is there?

I don't want to be questioned like this as if I was guilty of something.

Being crazy is not being guilty of anything. It's something you can't help.

Well, I'm not crazy.

Then you were lying.

I was lying.

Then I have a different ticket for you.

What is it this time?

A ticket to come with me to the police station.

What for?

For lying.

Arrest me for lying?

Sure.

Are you a policeman?

No.

Then how can you arrest me?

Because you're interested.

Interested! I'm horrified.

Then that's another name you go by. This definitely needs questioning by the police. You must be hiding something. You must have stolen a watch.

I stole nothing but my patience with you. I've taken too much.

This is a citizen's arrest. Come with me. You have confessed to lying, hiding under a pseudonym and stealing.

55.

In the spaces between the stars still water dances.
In the clouds of morning the evening is flowing
backwards to its evanescence—also meaningless to you.

I had not expected to convey to you my self
in transport in a vision, and now I must start again
to express it in yet another way, as the silent flower
in the silent desert that instantly begins to bloom
more silent flowers, as I am writing this.

Now you are surely in the desert there with me
because no such desert exists, we are
both at a loss. "This is my brother." I am
introducing you to the silent flowers,
and they understand.

56.

I wish a god were possible,
at least for me, to find myself
content in that knowledge
and as I die believe an immemorial mind
will hold me in remembrance live
and let to walk about
in an eternal sense of self,
as children do, looking up
into the sky, of which they sense
themselves a part, the sky boundless.
Children think so,
and in my wish for god, I am a child,
feeling in myself the wish
that is itself a god
in being boundless.

57.

"The waves laughed as they died."
Because they would be reborn
the moment they died.
They could laugh, like children
free of their parents on the open
streets of their happiness, to be
free to wander as life itself, as death:
two doors, neither of which would be marked,
and it would make no difference
to the children, the surprise to happiness
being to discover later which door
they had left behind
in their wandering.

58.

I am lifted from my sadness
to see everything as a gift
with which to make a life
that I could love
even as I lay dying. This
the religion I've been searching for
and now it is gone into this writing—
simply a hope and hope alone
to me is a reality but not to you
who have yet to feel
the need for hope.

59.

To welcome the day
from earliest creation
of the world, to spend himself
in adoration, to watch
the day depart in shades of darkness.
To speak of loss and of his faith
in day's return because of faith,
his world closed to evil
in this circle.

60.

The bull lunges at you!
Run, do not look back,
your hands, your mind vacant
with fear!

You make a stand,
whirl, and with hands on hips
lean towards the bull's eyes.
The animal wavers, snorts
and slows to a trot,
shaking his horns from side to side.
Still at a distance,
he turns away
to nibble grass.

But with his mind moved by his jaws,
he charges blindly,
once more to feel your eyes,
and lowers his head to the grass
at your feet.

61.

In sleep I meet myself,
and rise, as if awake,
to ride to work, and smile
at you who in that deep sleep
too ride with open eyes,
as if awake.

From every side we come
to meet our counterparts at work
asleep in their ecstatic love
of being.

62.

He sees the coming and going of friends
and adversaries and smiles to himself
of the secret he contains
of his complicity in living with the world
for he already knows the end
as he has known the beginning
but will live as in the beginning
until the end.

        He is that sort of schemer
and he adores himself as a smooth talker,
a friend to his foe and a friend to his own death.
He is happy without letting it be known
publicly because the odds are
that it would spoil the game of being alive
for to live is to think about it,
to draw conclusions, mainly skeptical
and reserved but to draw conclusions
that are in themselves works of art.

Happiness of that kind, reserved
for the privacy of his thoughts,
except for the others. Who are they?
He does not know but there are others
and they live, they live forever,
as he has been told by instinct
for living. In short, the world is not
about to end with him and there are the others
and he gives them his poems to keep,
as absentmindedly, distracted by life,
he walks off to his end.

63.

I've wanted to write my way into paradise,
leaving the door open for others too
to walk in. Instead, I am scribbling
beneath its walls, with the door shut.

What is the magic word?
Is there a magic word?
Am I standing beneath the walls of paradise?
Does paradise have walls?

Friends, strangers and relatives look to me
patiently or with sneers and amused tolerance,
crowding around, waiting for the door to open
at my words, but all I can offer are these
questions, and they see me uneasy, seated
with my back against the wall,
my eyes closed to rest, to sleep,
to dream of paradise
we were to enter at my words.

64.

It is wonderful to die amidst the pleasures I have known and so to die without recrimination towards myself and others, free of guilt at my shortcomings, happy to have lived and happy to know death, the last of living, my spirit free to sing as when I felt it born in my youth. The youth of it returns in dying, moving off from anger that racked its throat to make it sing with hoarse cacophony.

With death before me, I look back at my pleasures and they were you whom I held close in loving, and in the poems I've written for this truth, which is their beauty and lets me die in pleasure with myself. I did not fail my life.